Wonderings

Wonderings

*To Sheldon and Ann
With Much
love,
Roberta Meyer*

P.S. So glad you came out!

Roberta Meyer

Copyright © 2005 by Roberta Meyer.

ISBN :   Softcover   1-4134-9902-3

All rights reserved. No part of this book may be reproduced or transmitted in any form or by any means, electronic or mechanical, including photocopying, recording, or by any information storage and retrieval system, without permission in writing from the copyright owner.

This book was printed in the United States of America.

To order additional copies of this book, contact:
Xlibris Corporation
1-888-795-4274
www.Xlibris.com
Orders@Xlibris.com
29475

Contents

AMUSING

Poems 9
Woody Allen Moments 10
It Looks The Same To Me 11
Change 12
Poetry 13

NATURE

Birds Soar 14
Blue Heron 15
Daybreak 16
Mount Muzama and the Birth of Crater Lake 17
Mystic Miracles 19
Mystic Miracles 2 20
Mystic Miracles 3 21
Oh Pelican with Broken Wing 22
Alaska 23
Twilight Comes 24

SERIOUS

Sonnet 1 25
Debbie 26
Untitled 27
The Other Side 28
Forgiveness 29
Fragments 30
Gentle Love Lost 31
Juanita, My Friend 32
Megan 33
Memory 34
Small Hands 35
The Dance 36

The Problem 37
Was God Not There? 38
Anniversary 39

WORLD WAR II

Shellshock 1943 41
Adalia 1946 42
Day of Death 43
Patent Leather Shoes 45
Saki 46

SPIRITUAL

The Myth of Love 49
One Moment 50
Seasons 51
The Garden of Eden 52
The Second Coming 53

HAIKU

Haiku for Thor 55
Yellowstone Haiku 56
Grand Tetons Haiku 57
Grizzly Bear Haiku 58
Montana Haiku 59
Yukon Haiku 60
Dawn in Nopolo 61
Sunday 62

THOR'S PAGE

A Puppy's Favorite Things 65
Bicycle Ride 66
Everything's Different Now 67
A Day in Nopolo 68

Poems

Poems are stupid; they just don't make sense.
I can't understand them; I'm just way too dense.
So when the muse told me, "Roberta, my dear,
You're going to write poems," I made it quite clear
That to do so would mean all my life I'd been wrong,
And therefore, I'd prove that I didn't belong
To the intellects writing the verse of today
Who use words so fancy in all that they say.
But, nonetheless finding it fun to play games
With phrases and sounds and syllables and names
I gave myself over to writing a bit
Now I am hooked. I can't believe it!

Woody Allen Moments

My handbag catches on the door
Spewing contents everywhere.
I pitch forward, weirdly splayed
And find myself with graceless flair
In a Woody Allen moment.

Looking quickly all around
To see if I was spotted,
Alone, I hope, I do my best
To get myself unknotted
From my Woody Allen moment.

There's always lipstick on my teeth,
My slip is often showing,
I stumble into furniture
My clumsiness mind-blowing.
With talent so vast in one like me,
Who needs Mia or Diane?
I try to move with dignity,
I'm quite convinced I can,
Unless, of course, I'm in the grip
Of a Woody Allen moment.

It Looks The Same To Me

I look down and see the scurrying figures
Hurrying on their way.
They move with purposeful intention
Determined to reach their destination.
They have things to do and places to go.
I watch in fascination as their busy little bodies
Follow each other along the predetermined trail.
One or another occasionally deviates from the path.
Some appear confused, racing in circles.
Collisions occur. Important items are dropped or lost.
But, undeterred, they continue on their important way.
Driven by some compulsive need to survive,
They MUST carry that load,
They MUST achieve their goal.
It matters not if I am in Loreto
Gazing down on an anthill,
Or viewing New York City from a plane –
It looks the same to me.

Change

CHANGE IS GOOD, my sister said,
And she is right, I know.
I think it's quite good for my friends,
And often tell them so!
But when Fate throws a curve - at me -
And tells me I must alter
Some way I think, or tend to be,
I cringe and hide and cry and fight
With my entire mind and might.
Worn out by struggle, I then yield
And, as I've seen before, I find
By letting down my fearful shield
No longer am I blithely blind
To that which Fate has planned for me.
The Path is clear for me to see.

Poetry

I, too, could write – quite brilliantly –
Wise and graceful poetry
With phrases, flawless, and quite bold,
If I could use the words of old,
Words like "thou" and "thee".
My sounds so seamlessly would blend,
Such odes I'd pen if words like "ken"
Were available to me.
"Dost" and "Durst" would be my friends,
"Doth" and "Oft" I'd use freely,
Forgetting not the apostrophe!
For nothing serves a poet more
Than aids to rhythm and metaphor.
But writing poems in this day
Requires a different skill.
Careful to avoid cliché,
One still must fill the bill
Of writing profound thoughts so well
That all the critics go to 'ell.

Birds Soar

Above the azure sea of ruffling waves,
Birds soar and glide, then, kamikaze-like,
Dive head first into shimmering lagoons.
Emerging, triumphant, dinner in beak,
They shake their mighty wings, conquistadors
Of the sea, the sky, and all they survey.

Blue Heron

Blue heron, perfection poised upon one leg,
Lavender feathers stirring with grace,
Soft shades of peach and white revealed beneath.
Dignity projects from your regal face –
Crowned with stripes of black and silvered gray –
As you pose for us on your palapa perch,
One more gift in a delightful day.

Daybreak

Daybreak comes, a time I've rarely seen.
Now, purposely, I rise to welcome
The burnt orange sky.

I watch the coppered Sun
Stretch skyward.

Reaching for the heights of heaven
She moves – steadfastly – to reach
Her destination.

A life's lesson learned,
To stay the course, and let the day unfold;
The Sun's radiant path gives me strength untold.

Mount Muzama and the Birth of Crater Lake

Mount Muzama, mighty King of the Cascades
Your snow capped peak –
Thrusting majestically toward the heavens -
Towers above them all.

Your serene façade hides the torment within.
Angry eruptions –
Creating ever greater supremacy -
Embellish your mammoth size.

Ominous rumblings grow greater
As molten lava burns
Within the burbling cauldron of your soul.

And then, one day, explosive rage bursts forth.
Internal torment, expelled, destroys all in its path.
You, the mightiest mountain, cease to exist.

And yet, your demise, the catastrophe of eons,
Leaves a glorious legacy.
Your destruction brings forth unimaginable beauty.

Muzama, King of the Cascades, is destroyed.
And
Crater Lake, sapphire jewel of the Cascades, is born.

Mystic Miracles

In mystic magnificence,
Cumulus clouds crown
Majestic mountains
With crystalline coronets.
Legendary Lake Louise
Reflects the luminous sky,
Her glacial blue surface
Hiding secrets ancient and deep.
Glaciers glide in silent deceit,
Their lustrous forms descending
With relentless grace.
Apollo's glowing chariot illuminates the sky
Making the magical coronation complete.

Mystic Miracles 2

Marshmallow clouds in billowy shapes
Stretch across the endless sky.
White and gray masses of filmy fluff,
Encircled in shimmering silver,
Blanket the fragile world below.
Gazing down on farms with stately barns
Offering their gifts of shade and rain
They allow the sun, from her celestial throne,
To penetrate their filigreed forms
With iridescent shafts of quiet brilliance.

Mystic Miracles 3

Impenetrable granite penetrated,
Immovable boulders moved,
Marble crushed, trees trampled,
Earth torn, ripped, swallowed, and sliced
As inch by inch she uses her glacial force
To carve and sculpt a new world.
Her slow, methodical, relentless persistence
Creates destruction beyond imagination,
Leaving behind majestic mountains, glorious rivers,
Heavenly valleys, and magnificent lakes.
Should she be proud, or ashamed?

Oh Pelican with Broken Wing

Oh pelican with broken wing -
My heart aches as I watch you
Wandering up the concrete walk,
Bewildered by your helpless state.
How can it be that you no longer fly?

Why did you lose your freedom?
What dreadful sin did you commit
That caused your wing to tear,
Yet spared your friends who continue
In their soaring ease above you?

Why does one stumble while others climb?
How well I know the feeling.
The answer eludes me still.

Alaska

Glaciers calve for all to see
Mountain goats and elk are free
Wildflowers blossom everywhere
And Mount McKinley's over there
Mountains tower, streaked with snow
Glacial streams traverse below
Puffins fly beneath the sea
Black bears climb into a tree
Beavers build while otters play
Whales put on a grand display
Eagles soar, grizzlies roam
Alaskans call this heaven home

Twilight Comes

Twilight comes with cotton candy clouds
Wafting over lavender cliffs and cardboard cutout peaks.
Wispy shapes shift in shades of pink, peach, rose, and red,
Their crystalline borders brilliantly branding the heavens,
Their vermilion trails drifting to nowhere in particular.
Content with their destiny, these fated wanderers
Softly disappear as you take my hand.

Sonnet 1

The years have passed so quickly, don't you think?
How can we, still young at heart and full of zest,
Have children with lives on the very brink
Of loss, despair, and all that life can test?
Did I forget? Did we have heartache too?
Of course we did. There is no perfect life.
Yes, there were tears, and angry words that flew.
We've had our times of trouble and of strife.
And yet, I think the tumult of those days
Taught us that love, especially when shown
By laughing at our sometimes futile ways,
Confessing faults we might not want to own,
Brought us blessed forgiveness, strength and care.
And now, we're here – our silvered years to share.

Debbie

From the time she was small she lit up the world
With her chatter and humor and bright little ways.
Her teachers adored her, as did Mom and Dad,
And her six-year-old sister was ever so glad
To have a new playmate, especially a girl,
That she could now boss and tell what to do.
The day finally came. The younger one grew,
By-passing her sister by far.
Now, tall, statuesque, an attorney by trade,
Respected, admired and brilliant
There's only one thing that still makes her afraid
Her five-foot-tall sister, the tyrant!

Untitled

Quicksand – viscous, thick and unrelenting –
Pulls at the center of my darkened mind.
Rambling thoughts continue on fomenting
Dissension and distrust of every kind.
Every tool has failed so far to keep me
From the menacing depths so far below.
Freud and Jung were only temporary,
Although their wisdom caused the tides to slow,
And kept the shadowed blackness far away.
My fear is that this demon state will win.
I cannot seem to keep the grief at bay.
Is being depressed an illness or a sin?
Perhaps the answer, still a mystery,
Will soon be found and I will be set free.

The Other Side

There is the other side, of course.
The highs so high they transport my soul beyond the clouds.

Into the heavens I soar, to places I cannot envision.
And yet, I do.
I envision life, death, glory, grief, joy, and HEAVEN.
The greatest sorrows are filled with harmony,
Loss is blissful pain.
Elation aches, laughter weeps,
My body, leaving, sets me free.
Fulfillment reigns, until the reins of reality
Pull me back, back, back to this world
Where pain is pain, tears are tears, and despair is despair.

I grasp for euphoria. It eludes me every time.
And yet, I know the day will come when
I will live forever in the rapture of my soul.

Forgiveness

Perhaps to "forgive" means, "to give before".
If so, then give before what?
Perhaps to forgive is to acknowledge
The imperfections of human nature
Before they are revealed to us.

Do we fear that by forgiving we must forget?
Or is it possible that to forget
The fallible nature of being human
Is the only unforgivable act?

Fragments

Thoughts, in fragments, come and go at will inside my mind.
I cannot train them to behave; their dance is theirs alone.
If I could tell them what to do, I'd leave their grief behind
And fill my soul with joyous dreams, and feelings that enthrall.
Since that is clearly not to be, I live my life as if
I could, for all my hurtful words and wicked thoughts, atone.
Perhaps tranquility will come the day I fully know
My guilty sorrow will remain – 'til I embrace it all.

Gentle Love Lost

Gentle, joyous, blissful love
Danced into their lives that day.
So kind and sweet, with gracious care,
Their hearts spoke in a tender way.
The years have passed, and sorrows grate.
Now in their waning years they wait
For something that may never come.
Could it be that life, so brief,
Gives lessons to remember?
If they could bring the past to bear
On these, their autumn years,
Perhaps those special days of love
Could be theirs again – to share.

Juanita, My Friend

Juanita and I are so much alike – perhaps not to you,
Who see us from your own point of view.
But twins we are, in the depths of our hearts,
From the way we think to our love of the Arts.

Alike in looks? Oh no, not at all.
Juanita, petite with flashing brown eyes,
I, with blue eyes, blonde and quite tall.

She born in Chile, grew up riding horses
A ranch was her home.
I, northern born, danced in the City.
We met late in life, more is the pity.

But Providence reigns. Perhaps our late meeting
Is God's way of saying our lives, though fleeting,
Bring special gifts each step of the way.

Juanita, my friend, my care for you grows every day.

Megan

She was tiny and pink and her eyelids were graced
With lavender kisses the angels bestowed as they
Brought her from heaven to me.
The curl in her strawberry hair, soft and fine,
Rose like a crown on the top of her head.
Her cupid shaped lips curled up in a smile
Though the nurses said that could not be.
She was only a few hours old at the time
And they thought they knew better than me.
But I knew she was special the day she was born,
And this time I've been proven right.
She's my daughter, my friend, my petite confidant,
And I love her with all of my might.

Memory

Memory, remorse and misgiving,
All the frightful throes of living
That only one who's lived them knows,
Persisting yet in forward steps,
As though hell-bent on no repose.

Why so cruel to one's own mind?
What answers does one hope to find,
In such self-torture, such regret?
Do all who think much suffer so?
And, by such questions be beset?

The dawn may come, as life unfolds,
Revealing answers yet untold.
Repentant sorrow every day
Awaits the bless'd relief to come –
'Til then I go my burdened way.

Small Hands

Small Hands #1 Mexico
Small hands untie the bows on a brightly wrapped package.
Eyes widen, a smile breaks out.
It's a doll, or a truck, or a ball or a pretty pink lipstick.
Thirty children, one gift apiece.
Each gift is displayed for all to see.
The gift will be cherished, played with, used to a frazzled end
And then, passed on to a sibling or friend.

Small Hands # 2 USA
Small hands untie the bows on a brightly wrapped package.
Eyes expectant; smile, impatient.
One child, thirty gifts.
Dolls, trucks, balls, pretty pink lipsticks,
Each gift is quickly tossed aside
Perhaps with a perfunctory thank you, perhaps not.
Most will be used once or twice, then tossed into a closet, or a bin
Eventually to be given to the fire department.

The Dance

The dance begins with promise unburdened,
Filled with the delight of effortless motion.
Twirling, soaring, leaping, gliding,
All is freedom and escape.

Elation, ecstasy, escape –
That is the true promise of the dance.
Escape from life, escape from people,
Escape from struggle, escape from strife.

All is forgotten in the swirling bliss of the dance.

The Problem

Could it be that the problem is
That I don't want to be a problem?
Is my life about not wanting to be seen as
Intrusive
Selfish
Thoughtless
Irresponsible
Difficult
Temperamental
And a myriad of other unpleasant things?
Is my life then about trying to disprove a negative?
No wonder I'm so tired!

Was God Not There?

The earthquake came, and then the press,
And the people said, (those who survived)
"God Saved Me!"
The tornadoes ripped houses apart
And they told the press, (those who survived)
"It Was God's Will our lives were saved"
The hurricane, the worst ever,
Tore their homes to shreds
And they said (those who survived)
"Our Prayers Were Answered"
The kidnapped child was found
And they announced for all to hear
"We had faith that God wouldn't let us down"

And what of those who did not survive?
And what of those who were not found?
Was God not there for them?

Anniversary

Long love is like a marshmallow,
Soft and sweet, melted over glowing coals.
Long love is like pebbles in a stream,
Smoothly shaped by roiling rapids.
Long love is like iron,
Forged into strength by molten fire.
Long love is the best love of all.

Shellshock 1943

Julia's Dad was different from the other Dads.
First of all, he came to school every day to pick her up.
He always wore a suit, tie and hat.
He never uttered a sound.
And he shuffled – slowly.
Shuffle, shuffle, shuffle.
He shuffled through the schoolyard.
He shuffled up the steps to our classroom.
He looked around with blank eyes that seemed to see nothing.
But Julia always saw him.
She would run to him and throw her arms around his motionless body.
Then, one hand would rise slowly and pat her back, three times.
Pat, pat, pat.
Together they would leave the schoolyard.
Sometimes Julia would scamper ahead,
Sometimes she would put her small hand in his.
His hands scared me.
They were limp and much too white.
Shuffle, shuffle, shuffle.
Pat, pat, pat.
Sixty years ago, and the memory haunts me still.

Adalia 1946

Adalia is the only person I know with my exact birthday, date and year. But prior to our meeting at ballet class in summer of 1946 our lives had been quite different.

I was born in San Francisco on July 27, 1936.

Adalia was born in Manila on July 27, 1936

I was frightened by air raid drills and blackouts.

Adalia was frightened by wild monkeys.

My mother was forced to deal with my nightmares about soldiers hiding under my bed with bayonets

Adalia's mother was forced by soldiers with bayonets to watch as Adalia was caged with wild monkeys.

My mother, a nurse, took care of pregnant women whose husbands were away fighting the war.

Adalia's mother listened to pregnant women, about to deliver babies, screaming, as they died – hanging upside down.

I had freckles all over my face. Adalia had scars all over her body.

Where is Adalia today? Is she still scarred? I am.

Day of Death

He stumbled headlong through the trees – sweat streaming down his face.
The jungle roots caught at his boots, tripping him as he raced.
The body he carried was bloody and limp,
Weighing heavily on his slender frame.
And yet he moved with great intent, focused on his aim.
A medic set on saving lives, he took his mission seriously.
Today the stakes were very high. No ordinary soldier he.

When last I saw him I was young. He came to say goodbye.
Dark eyes and hair, slim and tall, he was so sweet to me.
Telling me stories that made me laugh, he sat me on his knee.
We joked and played as we had before, but something felt so strange -
Was it the uniform, or my mother's tone?
Cold fear swept over me.

To this day I cannot bear to think of how he died,
His best friend slung across his back. Shots rang out.
Steaming tendrils blocked him; he had nowhere to hide.
The bullet struck his burdened back. A sniper in a tree
Killed young Jimmy, and his friend, and reveled in the kill.
When my cousin died that day, so did a part of me.
Eight years old and filled with hatred for that coward in the tree.

Many say war is wrong and they may well be right.
Yet what is war, if not a ghastly fight? Perhaps
I should forgive the man who killed Jim so gleefully.
But I am not as good as that. If ever I meet him on the street,
He'd better run with all his might.
I'd drop him with a bullet and then ask him why
He shot Aunt Nita's only child in cold blood and let him die?
Do nightmares haunt him every night, as they did me?
If he answered "Yes", then perchance I'd set him free.
And this rage I've carried all my life would, perhaps, be gone from me.

Patent Leather Shoes

"What happened?" said the Teddy Bear to the Bunny by his side.
"We've been thrown out, for a pair of shoes!" Raggedy Ann replied.
The Bunny, lying on his face, could barely speak at all.
"I thought she loved us", he sadly sighed, glancing at Pretty Doll.
Pretty Doll was so upset all she could do was weep.
Her crinoline skirt, always so crisp, was lying in a heap.
"What did we do?" wailed Winnie the Pooh, looking for his honey.
Eeyore glumly glanced at his feet, mumbling, "Something's funny".

The little girl, just seven years old, having no thought that she
Could cause such hurt among her friends, went on obliviously.
Hugging her shoes, the glistening black shoes, she finally fell asleep.
She dreamed of places where she and her shoes could dance and prance
    and leap.
For years she had prayed for patent leather shoes, shiny Mary Janes,
And now they were here, pressed to her face. Her prayers were not in vain.
Her father, his coupons used for her, had no new shoes this year.
Though his soles were worn and the leather bare his choice was very clear.
And his little girl never forgot the gift from her Daddy Dear.

On the day she finally wore the shoes, the dolls and bunnies and bears
Came back to her bed where they knew they belonged, no longer in despair.
Forgiving the child for her young indiscretion, they cuddled as always
    before,
And the little girl learned that life could be good, even in times of war.

Saki

Saki was my summer Mom.
She took care of me at camp.
Camp was far, far, far away,
We drove for hours, it seemed to me –
Three hours is long for a child of two.
Of course, as Mama used to say,
"Roberta, you were ALMOST three,
And that was true.
The year was 1939,
June 16th, to be exact,
"We took the girls to camp today",
Said Daddy in his diary.
Were feelings there? I never asked.
Perhaps I didn't want to know.
I don't remember the first days –
We stayed all summer long –
But Saki I remember well.
There were six in my small group,
"Out of diapers" was the rule.
I was the babe, and all the rest
Were three or four years old.
Although I thought she loved me best
I'm sure she loved us equally.
And she was our security.

She took us in the little boat,
And taught us how to swim.
Sometimes she let us stay up late,
To join the "big kids" singing songs.
The campfire blazed and warmed our toes,
Melted marshmallows stuck to our chins.

When finally we went off to bed
She'd tuck us in, give us a kiss,
And help us say our prayers
Each time my prayer was just the same,
"Let them come and take me home tonight."
I wouldn't close my eyes at all,
For fear I'd miss them when they came,
But Saki, sitting by my side,
Would gently stanch the flowing tears
And calmly hold my little hand
Until my heavy eyelids closed.
I came to love her, oh so much,
And as I grew and the years passed
I could hardly wait for summertime
To see my Saki once again.
And then, one year, she wasn't there.
Bewildered, I searched through the camp.
It could not be as they told me.
"Saki won't be here this year."
If she loved me as I loved her,
Then surely she'd return.
The summer dragged on, endlessly,
My heart, betrayed, all joy gone,
And there was no one there this time
To gently stanch the flowing tears.
It was years before I learned why
My Saki couldn't be with me.

She, too, had been sent off to camp,
For having made just one mistake -
Her eyes, you see, were the wrong shape.
And all the people with those eyes,
And slightly different colored skin,
Were sent away for four long years.
When she returned, I gave her hugs
And told her how much she was missed.
But now, at eight, I was too old
To be in Saki's special group.
I was now one of the "big kids".
And so, at five, (well, almost six)
I lost my childlike innocence.
The world was harsh and full of loss,
Nonetheless I'll not forget
Those memories of Saki's gentle love.
They still stand me in good stead.

The Myth of Love

If love is a feeling, then where does it go
When anger overtakes me?
When I don't *feel* loving, then how do I know
That my love did not simply flee?

It's said, "You just KNOW", but I must know how
Because I'm completely aware
How my mind can easily disavow
Those things I'm unwilling to share.

Love as a choice may not be expedient
Or easy, or sweet, or just plain convenient.

Yet making a choice does not appeal
If it means I must stay when I want to leave,
Or say things that really are real.
So then what IS love? It is this, I believe.

Wanting the best is love at its zenith,
And that is the option I find I must choose.

If I am unwilling to forfeit the myth
I'm not free to love with nothing to lose.

One Moment

One moment, out of time,
Changed my life forever.
My spirit soared, weightless, unconstrained.
I knew only one thing.
I was free, wondrously free.
I missed no one.
I wished for nothing.
In that one awesome moment
Every choice in the universe
Was available to me,
And I could choose, freely.

Seasons

I want to be born like an innocent bud
Bursting forth in the Springtime air.
I want to live life like a Summer breeze
Traveling everywhere.
I want to die like the Autumn leaves
Blazing in vibrant hues,
Then I'll rest under Winter's soft snow
Cradled by Earth, my Muse.

The Garden of Eden

Could this be it?
Could *this* be the Garden of Eden?
Perhaps we simply forgot
When we learned of duality.

If we could forget again,
If we could forget
We ate from the Tree,
The Tree of Knowledge of
Good and Evil,
And could willingly give up
Our arrogant reading
Of God's mind,
Perhaps our innocence would return
And all would seem to be
Not only the way it is,
But exactly the way
It ought to be.

The Second Coming

What if the second coming has already come?
What if the second coming means seeing the
Christ
Within? What if there is no outward sign
But just an inward sense
That we must live our lives as though
God
Were with us. Never gone, always there to guide us.
Would we hear
God's
Word if there was nothing else to hear?
And would we abide by that voice inside?
Or continue on our facile way,
Pretending we had no idea of
God's
Will for us?
What kind of courage would it take
To risk all that we think we know,
To let go of old ideas others taught us.
To follow that voice, as a child of
God,
With
Christ
As our example?
Standing in the face of those
Who think they know the answers
Without an argument; no way to prove
We are RIGHT.

Are we willing to be betrayed by Friends and Justice,
With no recourse but
God?
Are we willing to be crucified?
Are we willing, unlike martyrs do,
To act, be, and believe – and take the consequences
Without invoking the name of
God?
Will we pray inside our home and heart
Instead of kneeling publicly
For all to see.
Will we agree NOT to
Defend our actions as the will of
God?
Will we judge not the other? And yet
Tell the truth of what we see,
Not self righteously
Though it cost us our life? If
Christ
Lives in us, then we have no excuse for cowardice.
But as long as
Christ
Is without, as long as we are still "seeking"
Christ
We can excuse almost anything.
However if we choose to believe that
Christ
Has already come again, and truly lives in us, then
We have no choice
But to live our lives courageously.

Haiku for Thor

Little one so sweet
When God gave me such a treat
Life began anew

Tiny puppy, Thor,
Gentleness that I adore
Come to Mommy now

My soft cuddly boy
Never had I such a toy
In my entire life

Feisty little guy
Stubborn, too, if I may say!
You *will* have your way

Puppy so complete
Huge brown eyes and precious feet
You bring joy to me

Yellowstone Haiku

Glistening rivers
Run amongst the stark burnt trees
Yellowstone destroyed

Steaming vents burst forth
Valiant young trees reach for sun
Yellowstone reborn

Grand Tetons Haiku

Grand Tetons rising
Framed by copper colored trees
Lakes reflect in awe

Grizzly Bear Haiku

Rambling grizzly bear
Soft and cuddly you appear -
How one's looks deceive

Montana Haiku

Brilliant golden trees
Line the soft velvet meadows
Mountains climb above

Gentle rivers flow
Then turn to roiling rapids
Azure lakes appear

Yukon Haiku

Milky blue river
Cascading through the valley
From the glacier born

Dawn in Nopolo

Haiku

Iridescent sea
Reflecting luminous clouds
Dawn in Nopolo

Cumulous puffs lined
With brilliant peach neon stripes
Dawn in Nopolo

Celestial blue sky,
Billowing marshmallow shapes
Dawn in Nopolo

Sunday

Haiku

Soft serene Sunday
Glorious God given gift,
Rest, respite, repose.

THOR'S PAGE

A Puppy's Favorite Things

Cuddling with mom, climbing on dad,
Running on grass, chewing a chew,
These are my favorite things to do.
But there are many others too.

Going out to dinner makes me glad.
Steak or chicken? I don't care,
As long as my folks take me there.
(Being left at home is so unfair!)

Playing with friends is special, too.
And family is the best of all,
Mikey, Deb, and Craig —so tall!
And then there's Meg, like me, so small.

All these things make life complete.
Some say I'm "spoiled", but I think not.
The joy I bring is quite a lot.
I'm sure I've earned all that I've got!

Bicycle Ride

"Time to go," She says, with her perky look,
I act like I'm sleeping, Dad stares at his book.
She puts on her hat, and that silly bag
She carries me in, and, trying not to nag,
She urges us to climb on the bikes
And head down the palm-lined road.
Dad moans as his legs ache and complain,
Mom peddles on with me as her load
Refusing to tell Dad she too is in pain.
But, once on our way, if I let it be known,
I start to enjoy the ride. Such smells and sights,
Remind me the world is full of delights.
My whines tell Mom to let me run on my own.
I lope, and gallop and prance on the grass,
And once we are home,
Dad sits on the deck sipping his drink
I lie, curled up in my bed, and think,
Sometimes when I do something that may not seem fun
The rewards are worth it – once its done!

Everything's Different Now

We went to Ukiah for a nice drive –
And everything's different now.
A day in the country with people I love,
And everything's different now.

With Mom at the wheel, I sat on Meg's lap;
She petted and hugged me. She gave me kisses.
But everything's different now.

We stopped at a Denny's. I glanced outside.
I saw the small puppy, and I almost died.
Black with tan markings and short little legs,
In the arms of a woman I knew.
Her name is Linda, (the lady who brought him),
I'm thankful she gave me to Mom,
But it never entered my mind
That she had another, (they say he's my brother),
And everything's different now.

Megan adores him. Mom thinks he's cute.
Meg named him "Rocky", just right for a brute!
Although they betrayed me, I guess I'll adjust.
Meg still wants to play and it looks like I must,
But not with HIM, who barged into my life,
Changing my status as King.
Well, Mom says she'll always love *me* most of all.
And Dad says, in his life, I'm the very best thing;
Still, everything's different now.

A Day in Nopolo

I wake in the morning as sunlight streams in,
Depositing sunspots galore.
I choose the best, knowing I'll stay
At least as long as I wish.
I'll then move on to the next perfect place
While Mom and Dad sit on the deck.
They stare at the sea, sipping coffee
Lost in a Nopolo Stupor.

The day proceeds slowly. We don't have to rush -
We're living on Mexico time.
We go for a bike ride, have lunch and a nap,
Awaking, we have sweets, and tea.
And now we may stroll on the beach or the path.
The desert surrounds us, and mountaintops soar,
As the Sea of Cortez, azure and clear,
Wraps her lagoons around us.

Returning home, we sit on the deck
Enfolded in twilight's embrace.
Dinner Time comes, and I get some treats,
Then Dad and I play on the bed.
Bunny and Wolf, my favorites still,
Get chewed and mauled and chased.
Mom hides the bone, I find it and she,
Impressed by my skill, kisses me.

Mom and Dad read for a while, and then
It's time to say goodnight.
We curl up together, Dad, Mom and I
And off to dreamland we go.
Knowing our dreams, no matter how sweet,
Will never surpass a day in Nopolo.

Edwards Brothers Malloy
Thorofare, NJ USA
March 18, 2014